MW01593591

200 Months of Rain
SPOKEN WORDS BY LAMONT

200 Months of Rain
SPOKEN WORDS BY LAMONT

— LAMONT —

Nashville, TN

200 Months of Rain
By Deon Tolliver
Copyright © 2010 by Deon Tolliver

ISBN 13: 978-0-9826694-1-9

Published by
True Vine Publishing Company
P.O. Box 22448
Nashville, TN 37202
www.TrueVinePublishing.org

Printed and bound in the United States of America.

For more information about the author or the book, contact True Vine Publishing, P.O. Box 22448, Nashville, TN. 37202 (615) 585-0143

Dedicated to my Savior and Inspiration.
Thank you for being better to me than I have been to myself.

Table of Contents

Inspired

The thought of you inspires me,
To live in R.E.M. sleep.
The light at the end of the tunnel is a thing to see.
Inspired not to give up,
Inspired to be me.
Inspired to overcome all negativity
The name calling and feelings of inadequacy.
Inspired to make you know
There is more to me than what you can see
And you can't find out unless you're inspired to see it.
The thought of you inspires me
Like when a smile pierces your lips
And how I can see all your teeth.
The thought of your walk and that little skip you do
Inspired by how you talk.
You're something to praise but remain humble.
Inspired by you because you make me better
Never have you ever let me settle.
And I would do the same for you
Along with inspire, cherish, nurture, and honor you.
The thought of you inspires me
To grow roots into your thought patterns for eternity.
Inspired to remain for the better, even during the worst
Until we make our last encore in matching hearses.
I'm inspired to make all your fears a figment of your imagination
The thought of you inspires me
To create a love as strong as the Pacific is deep
Inspired to be patient
Inspired not to be cheap
Inspired to build you up with the words I say
Never tear you down, no time, no situation, no way
Inspired by the things hoped for and not seen
Inspired by the thought of you and me.

Timelessness

I have loved you forever in one lifetime.
If I don't live another second, I'll be satisfied.
Basking in the leftover remnants of your love
Laughing hysterically
at the jokes you would have eagerly told.
It wouldn't matter if the jokes weren't funny
Or if you didn't have a pet name for me like "Sweet thang,"
"Sugar Pie" or "Honey."
Just be there. A covering.
Shield me from hurt, pain, and disappointment always.
If you were mine, I would love you
every second of every hour, EVERY way.
Searching the past and reevaluating the present
to arrange my thoughts
To think of new ways to love you with all my heart.
I would never underestimate you or take you for granted.
And never forsake the seeds of intimacy that we've planted.
Be patient, God is not through with me yet.
Molding a better man through blood, tears, and sweat.
It seems like days are nights and nights are days,
Timelessness,
lost in your eyes and the freckles on your face
Brown skin the color of cinnamon
Without blemish, because I didn't take the time to scrutinize
your faults.
Perfection in all of its glory,
Every scar, every extra tooth, and every chin.
Time wouldn't allow me to tell this story
Time is irrelevant, our love would never end.

Alone

If you really loved me, you wouldn't have left so fast.
What?
You don't remember what you said as we lay tangled between
the sheets in bed?
And please don't tell me it was the heat of the moment,
because that's more than my heart can bear.
Looking intensely at the walls
and they return cold, hard stares.
Because you left me. Alone.
What happened to talking on the phone for hours, when you
couldn't wait to hear my voice?
Now after a few minutes you have to go or you don't answer
at all. It's your choice.
I wish you would have given me the option to choose,
Instead of the "my wife and dog left me" blues.
I should have used my other head and seen it coming from
some of the stuff you said like,
It's not the same, and you don't know who to blame, and
You're no longer excited about the relationship.
I was too busy trying to work on our relationship.
Trying to fix something that was beyond repair,
Putting duck tape around my heart,
trying to hold it together
I searched your eyes relentlessly for some sign of love and
found nothing. Not even a little bit.
No restrained emotion yearning to come outside like a little
kid. Where did it go?
When you left me. Alone.
With nobody to care
because they're too busy doing their own thing.
A dictionary couldn't describe this hurt and pain.
I feel mutilated, mauled, mangled and maimed.
damaged, destroyed and drained.
That's how you left me. Alone.

Desire

Can you believe how our love has grown?
To a harvest to be reaped after all the seeds we've sown.
Ever know what it means to need someone.
What's your number not being dialed by my phone?
That's nothing short of a catastrophe,
Like the whole world getting chicken pox
At the same time is an anomaly.
Different colored roses could barely convey my emotions.
It's like warm blood over the fangs of a werewolf
It's ferocious!
And I wouldn't usually say this, but outside of you,
I have no wants.
My needs were met with your smile,
my desires were manifested in your walk.
Should I be selfish and keep you to myself
Or should I let the world know?
Thank God for you, my blessing.
You're how His love for me is shown.
My desire for you can't be matched nor tamed.
It can't be denied and it can't be named.
Supposedly, the average heart beats 35 million times every
365 days.
Mine beats more than that when we hold hands.
Desire for you has me speechless and blinded,
Infatuated with your love and absent minded.
Let's not forget to be the people we have always been.
Lovers laughing at the thought of not being friends.
You can't be described with all the words in all the books in
all the world.
So most of the time, I just call you "Pretty Girl."
Let's cherish this thing called love through the fire.
Let's be each other's desire.

Don't Cry for Me

If I should die before I wake,
And can't repent before my soul is taken,
As long as my life is in His hands,
I have no fear of death or man.
If I become a quadriplegic with HIV and then AIDS,
And put X's on my calendar to count down the days
Don't cry for me.
If my plane goes down in a catastrophic burning inferno,
If I go skiing and get buried alive under the snow;
I love this life and the things it has to offer,
But for Paradise, I would put a down-payment on my coffin.
Don't cry for me.
If my kid's school bus hydroplanes off a cliff
Don't cry for them either
Because they escaped a bunch of nonsense.
If I go out dancing with my wife
And we get killed by a drunk driver that night
Don't cry for us because we'll be with the Lord
Free! from the ridicule, stress, deceit, and bills in this world.
So don't cry for me.
No need of tires for my car or money for my braids,
No standing in long lines Christmas shopping
for other people on Jesus' birthday
I won't have to see the ungrateful look on one face.
I won't have to hear what I'm not doing right
or what people have to say.
My leather Lazy Boy is waiting in Paradise.
I hope He doesn't hold the things I did in this life against me.
I am not ready to die, I just have no fear
Don't cry for me, cry for the people left here.

A Beautiful Mind

Do you remember telling me
the average person blinks 5,000 times a day?
Where do you get your information
That people soak up like sponge cake?
I love to watch TV with you,
especially Jeopardy and Family Feud.
You're the only one who can make me laugh
About my mother looking like a dude.
I stay on the phone with you all night
knowing I have to go to work
Just to be enlightened and hear you make up words
Into sentences I don't quite understand.
But you don't hesitate to explain things in
layman's terms for this simple man.
Who else cares why the elephant
is the only animal with four knees
I fell in love with your over-analytical side.
You should have been a comedian from how you
have me hurting in my side from laughter.
Even if you don't know what you're talking about
and forget what you're saying,
And your $100,000 words escape your brain
before reaching your mouth.
If you say it like you mean it, I'd bet my house on it
Because of your beautiful mind.
If you were in a bad accident and became a vegetable,
I'd stay by your side at the hospital forever,
And watch the brain waves from the machine on the table.
If there weren't any waves, I'd stare at a lifeless line,
And reminisce about your beautiful mind.

Anxious

That's what it's made for.
Is what I thought for so long.
If I couldn't have the real thing
I would settle for it over the phone.
And even though the attraction between us is so strong,
it's wrong.
Or is it?
I can't say.

Forgive me for being anxious.
For my actions, I have no words.
My anticipation soars higher than all reason free as a bird.
Mostly because of the honesty that we have.
Hopefully that's not a figment of my imagination.
I hope the line that we've crossed
Doesn't force us apart.
I hope the look in your eyes
Still shines and sparkles.
Forever more, I'll try not to be anxious.

Just Be There

With a smile radiating happiness
And lips begging to be kissed
If I felt anything other than anxious
I would be remiss.
I've thought of you nonstop since
Last in your warm embrace.
Dreaming about you is only enough
To make me yearn to be in your presence.
You wouldn't have to know I was there.
Tell me you love me or return my stares.
Just be there.

Can You See

We all want to hear what we want to hear,
But the truth is a hot topic.
Sin has been brewing like stew
on the stove in a Hell-sized pot.
Some people are perfect and beyond reproach.
The rest of us need His help
Before we get burned by the stove.
The stew tastes good for the meantime;
"I'm not as bad as I could be"
Lord have mercy on our souls
When you show us the error of our ways
And we act like we can't see.

Trust

The more I trust, the more control I lose.
What? I don't have control?
I knew that, I ain't no fool.
But I built a wall anyway.
Something like a defense mechanism or disguise
To conceal my disappointment from treachery and lies.
If I trust with all my heart then what's left for me?
Such a small word to have such a big meaning.
Does that mean I need faith?
Some little girls trust their fathers and end up being raped.
You said it's better to put confidence in the Lord
than in man.
If I can't trust people, what kind of life do I have?
It's not that I don't trust; it just takes a while.
Like two hundred months to build up
And two seconds to tear down.

Guilt-free Sex

Baby, I love you and I know you love me too.
Why can't we just do what we want to do?
I'll use a condom.
If you don't like that, I'll pull out in enough time.
Just relax, the withdrawal method works fine.
I won't tell anybody you let me get it.
I'm not like the others who just want to hit it and quit it.
You're always talking about "it's not right,
We need to be married"
And things being done in God's sight.
If God didn't want me to have you,
He wouldn't have made you so fine.
What's a little guilt?
It's not like it's casual sex. You're already mine.

You must be crazy talking about, "The withdrawal method
works just fine."
I'm not thinking about getting pregnant. I'm thinking
about a fatherless child.
Do you want to put a ring on my finger?
I'm not worrying about what you tell?
Will you go with me through the fire
Or lead me straight to hell?
What happens if it's not good or you finish too fast?
Then I'm stuck with something that will last. Guilt.
It's not right in God's sight, and the fact that you don't
agree raises a red flag.
Be patient and stop trying to get it so bad.
Are we on the same page, because
I want to be intimate and you want to have sex.
Don't get me wrong, I like having sex too; it's the way he
made me.
I just want to do it and be guilt-free.

You Make Me Wanna

You make me wanna sing that Usher song
Leave the one I'm with and start a new relationship
And not just 'cause you supafly and know how to use a whip.
But because your smile lights up my life 33 different ways
And I could live off a few seconds of your laughter for 7
months and 3 days.
You make me wanna rip my heart right out of my chest
Serve it to you on a silver platter
and not worry about the rest.
You make me wanna grab you and pull you close
Hold you forever, kiss your lips and right above your nose.
You make me think things I'd be reluctant to ask
but burning to know.
I wonder if you think about me in your dreams,
or on your way to work.
You make me wanna get some instructions
about how love is supposed to be
So I could give it to you relentlessly.
You make me wanna study you
and forget everything I ever learned
Except how to write and love
So I could put it in a poem.

Jealous

I don't want you with him or her, even though you're not mine.
That takes away from me. Time after time.
There are no explanations for the feelings of inadequacy.
You never told me you wanted me.
As a matter of fact, you said that I was too young,
too broke, and too care-free.
It's still hard to conceal my jealousy.
We used to go to lunch together
and you would call me periodically.
Now you don't even come by and barely speak to me.
It's like I don't exist. Why'd you change?
And I'm not the only one that sees me
Trying hard to hide my jealousy.
Is it something I said or something I did
That made you put me in the corner like a little kid?
Now someone else is making you laugh
And I can't do anything but sit back, chill out, and laugh
To mask my jealousy.
Would it mean anything if I told you how I feel?
I can't do that.
Charity attention would be worse than before. For real.
God, how can You allow me to feel like I do?
"I had to my child, to let you know I feel just like you
Trying to conceal my jealousy."

My Heart/My Conscience

My heart is telling me to love that man.
My conscience is telling me to stay where I am.
And even though I'd be provided for
and not have a care in the world
Only thing I need is love, I'm a simple girl.
Being married is like tasting food
that's not as good as it sounds
I could still be lonely and experience an emotional drought.
Being single is even worse.
It's like digging for something
Lost in the bottom of an empty purse.
That doesn't mean hastily rush into things
But I'm not getting any younger
and my patience is becoming thin.
My heart is telling me I love that man.
My conscience is telling me to stay where I am.
My man is constantly on the road
and my friend is around all the time.
I'd do almost anything to be happy for just a little while.
I don't have to be alone.
What's wrong with kickin it with my friend?
I know he will "try me" but I always have fun with him.
Why move to a place
where no one knows my name
Just to be with a man
who might expose me to hurt and shame?
He might make me happy all the days of my natural life
And I could be a loving mother and supportive wife.
That sounds nice.
Right now I'm just a little confused.
What's wrong, what's right, what should I do?
My heart is telling me I love that man.
My conscience is telling me to stay where I am.

Let Me Go

You acted like you didn't want me when you had me.
Now all of a sudden my worth you see.
Should I believe you, again
And confide in my friends?
"He's different this time, plus I love him so much."
I don't really care what they think. But
I refuse to be a fool, a homie-lover-friend
And be your play thing, again.
And get my hopes up so high
Only to be shot out the sky
Act like you did before, like I didn't exist.
Just let me go.

I didn't know that I had you.
You intentionally made yourself so hard to love.
If we were worth so much, you wouldn't let me know
How quick and fast you could let me go.
I didn't act like you didn't exist
until the good times disappeared.
I would have let you go a long time ago
If I knew things would end like this.

Lord Have Mercy

Lord have mercy on my soul
As I go through life anxiously pursuing goals.
Not giving You the proper amount of respect or time
And complaining when Your plans conflict with mine.
Forgive me for acting mad at You that day
When I asked You for some answers
and You told me to wait.
Only You knew that I wasn't ready for it
Five years later still finding me and not ready for it.
Lord, have mercy on my soul
When I wake up and don't pray before
School and work.
And I know in every corner how dangers lurk
I don't want to be broke
so I put up with the crazy people at work.
Allow me to pass every test in life
with wisdom my mind has gathered.
When the time is right, don't let my thoughts be scattered.
If I would have known then what I know now,
I would have asked for mercy long before now.
I thought I didn't know how.
Lord have mercy on my soul
If I don't come to You like I did before.
I haven't forgotten about the day You saved me
Or the many times You kept me from the grave either.
I do love you even though I don't show it.
Your grace is what kept me from really blowing it.
You had mercy on me when I was doing the wrong thing
And You threw my sins into the depths of the sea
when I did it again.
Lord have mercy.

Love

Words couldn't describe it and actions wouldn't show
How with every second that passes,
our love steadily grows.
This love doesn't ignite and die out with the fire of passion.
This love is miraculously abundant,
Unaltered by my lack of enthusiasm.
You told me you would never leave me or forsake me.
I believe you, because you keep all Your promises.
With no strings attached and no drama comes with it.
Well, maybe a little but you love me no matter what I do
Knowing the same wouldn't be done for you.
Even though I lied to you and I was dead wrong.
You opened Your heart and spread wide Your arms,
To cover me with love so divine
I'm right in the middle of it
And can't comprehend it with my mind.
Our love crosses state lines, hemispheres and time zones;
Heals past wounds, shattered dreams and broken homes.
I don't have to guess if You love me,
It's shown in so many ways.
You're always there when I need You
And I don't have to beg You to stay.
You are the rain to grow my food,
And the sun to brighten my day.
I know You told me a million times
but I love to hear You say
Your love is patient and kind
and You'll never take it away.
You don't have to buy me stuff or make my pockets fat.
I'd rather read Your love letters, nothing's better than that.

Mixed Emotions

Are you with me or against me?
I have to ask because sometimes I get confused.
And don't start acting funny when I tell you this or get
things misconstrued,
But, you're sending me mixed messages
in what you say and what you do.
When we met, you said you only wanted to be friends,
But you would feel me up and down
like a blind man with six hands.
And I don't understand how you want me,
But you're not ready for a commitment.
And you took a key to my apartment with no hesitation
and very little resistance.
You say you love me but you're not in love with me.
The look in your eyes tells it all.
When you hold me so tight, all my problems seem so small.
I'm cliffhanging off the words your mouth has in store,
either wonderful sweet nothings
Or curse words that tear me down from the pedestal you
put me on just two seconds before.

Mixed Emotions pt.2

You took me out for my birthday and brought me flowers.
Then you didn't return my calls
for five days and ten hours.
I asked why you didn't call and you said I was overreacting
as usual and we needed time apart.
I guess you didn't get enough attention where you were because
you came back and told me I would always have a
special place in your heart.
Your smile comforts me
but your words cut like broken glass.
Your voice soothes me
until you bring up something from the past.
Why are you still calling my mother's house
and asking to speak to my little girl?
Only to leave us high and dry
Once let into our world.
For some reason, I can't let you go,
I keep letting you back in,
As much as you hurt me.
I don't know why I still think we can be friends.

No More Pain
(Inspired by Wesley Rice, Sr.)

I thank God because
He has no more pain
No need for earthly things and no room for shame.
No one to point a finger and no one to blame.
Thank You Jesus because
He has no more pain.
Everybody will say "He's in a better place."
Because we know that a sad tear shouldn't touch our face.
But tears of joy because we know he's in paradise.
Granddad, we love you so much and celebrate your life.
If we didn't say it enough while you were here
It doesn't matter now.
We thank the only One we can that he has no more pain
No need for earthly things and no room for shame.
No one to point a finger and no one to blame.
Thank God our love has no more pain.

Off Limits

Loving you is wrong but I don't want to be right
And if we're not supposed to be together,
I can't tell.
The look in your eyes says it all
Making me intrigued, wondering your most intimate
thoughts.
The fact that I have a girlfriend brings all that to a halt.
But she doesn't know how you smell
Or why you make me feel like you do
Just from a smile.
And if she knew how you felt....
She would want you too.
For now you're off limits.
And there's nothing sweeter than forbidden fruit.
DANGER! STAY AWAY!
Pay attention to the signs.
Because when I'm around you, I lose my mind.
But your attractiveness goes a lot deeper than your body.
I want to make love to your mind.
Controlling myself is halfway possible to do
If I wanted to.
"Off limits" is a phrase I never wanted to use to describe
you.

One Million Years

Never knew in a million years
That a life boat would come in the form of you
To bring me to the safety found in love.
I know you were sent from some extra terrestrial place.
Because never in a million years
Has my tongue stopped working like when you appear.

Never knew in a million years
I'd be here with you, wiping away your tears.
And it's not as bad as it might sound
I would use the salt from your tears to season my food
If that was the only way I could have you around.

Happy Mother's Day

I know money can't buy your love,
so I have no gift cards or jive
I decided to make you a grandmother
before you turn thirty-five.
All of the time and effort you put into me is paying off well.
Does it really matter that I had to spend a little time in jail?
You never turned your back on me and always showed love.
May God bless you with all the gifts He has above.
When I'm rich, I'll buy you a big house
with a porch in the shade.
But for now, I'll just say, "Happy Mother's Day!"

The Devil Is A Liar

The devil is a liar if he thinks he can fool me.
My momma always said
If you resist him, he will flee. (James 4:7)
But it's not easy.
He prowls around like a roaring lion
looking for someone to deceive (1 Peter 5:8)
With counterfeit miracles, signs and wonders (2 Thess. 2:9)
Telling me "It's alright to do/say it"
Then torment me with a guilty conscience
And only for his fun
Does he make me think God won't deliver.
Hope, trust and love he snatches away.
The ancient serpent the devil,
who leads the world astray (Rev 12:9)
Got people using people, playing the game the devil's way.
Lord save us from the accuser
Because earthly pleasures feel so good.
But only for the moment, then the guilt kicks in.
If he can't get us to procrastinate,
he'll get us to compromise.
Hatred is his daughter and he's also the father of lies.
(John 8:44)

Too Much for Herself

A delectable novelty, never to be denied
Her walk made my thoughts stand in time.
That's why words can't describe that "5 '9, light brown with
the same color eyes.
The totality of her is far beyond her thighs
It reaches further than the kitchen. Passion is her guide.
Bred to be a scholar,
Einstein must be in the lineage of her parents
Her intelligence is radiant and free of arrogance.
Bred to be a Stallion, magnificently made
and too much for herself,
I didn't know she was a doctor.
I thought she was straight off the shelf
Out of some magazine.
What was God thinking when He gave her those lips,
That untamed spirit and those voluptuous hips
That always seem to steal the scene?
Her body is it. But her enthusiasm about life
is what mesmerizes me.
On the outside she's hard and on the inside, so sweet.
Simple, yet sophisticated, and I swear in all my days
Never have I ever admired a woman this way.

When It Hurts So Good/Blame It on the Rain.

You make my mouth drop and drool
Everyone can see I look like a fool.
You showed me it was possible to hurt so good,
The crazy things I've done for your love
will never be understood.
I'll try not to bring up your cheating again,
The kids shouldn't see us fight anymore
Now that I've stopped yelling so much, I feel crippled, but
my throat is no longer sore.
Though we've gotten perfect at pointing the finger
And so bad at bearing the shame,
Let's not argue tonight, let's blame it on the rain.
We made so many good memories
in the past 12 years and 8 months, but
Somebody else had to hold me when I flunked my boards
and lost our son in the same month.
Don't worry about cursing me out,
You made up for it with the dinner and flowers.
I wasn't really trying to kill you
when I threw that plugged-in radio in the shower.
The bad memories would disappear
if you loved me how I love you.
Then we could fall asleep on the beach
and hold hands at the zoo.
We can't even agree on where to go
Let alone decide on what to see at the show.
I love you with all my heart, but can't stand you sometimes
And I can't figure out why I'm still with you to save my life.
So since I don't understand my own brain
When it hurts so good, just blame it on the rain.

Why Me/Thank You

Some call it luck, but I call it favor.
I must have really been messing up if I needed a Savior.
Because You chose to save me
from the depression and disgrace.
I have a healthy amount of pride
and don't have to hide my face.
Who would have thought
that the little child down on his knees
Would dare to achieve his wildest dreams.
That's why I only rest enough to keep going,
and when I'm dog tired
In my deliriousness, I thank You
for giving me my heart's desires.
For accepting me in school
and seeing me through graduation
And for making me the supervisor
of people who are more qualified and twice my age.
Why do You want me to change the world?
I can barely change myself.
Why do You keep me from feeling shame
when I say something crazy and embarrass both of us?
I could have been a raped widow,
slain after my husband and children in Sudan,
Or a slave, a molested child,
or a victim of terrorist attacks by the Taliban.
I couldn't have done anything to deserve it;
so why do You bless me like this?
You saved me from generational curses
of crack, abuse, poverty and prison.
You gave me hope, provided for me,
and kept me from it ALL.
My wonderful, awesome, Healer and King,
the One who is able to keep me from falling.
When I ask "why me" I'm not complaining,
I just don't want to disappoint You.
Between me and You,

I am afraid of failing and looking like a fool.
As You keep blessing me,
I'm going to bless others until I run out of time
Because none of this is for me.
It's for Your glory.
And that's why I thank You

Y'all Just Don't Know

Y'all just don't know
I was praying and fasting and even gave up sex,
Studied day and night to pass that funky test.
If I would have just let the Dean have a peak at my hall pass,
I probably would have been in school quick and fast.
Or been played like a fool with no dignity and no class.
They've let people in with scores the same as my shoe size
But they wouldn't let me in, now my life I despise.
Because being in the Class of 2012 has been my life
Y'all just don't know
I thought about taking my life.
Then there would be no shame to bear
and I wouldn't have to pass a test.
I wouldn't have to worry about my future,
I wouldn't have to explain the rest.
People keep calling and giving me there condolences
With every call I get closer to the edge of the cliff,
Just push me over it.
Everybody keeps saying,
"God didn't bring me this far to leave me"
God left me a long time ago, and even I couldn't believe it.
Y'all just don't know.
About the pressure I have on me to succeed.
Failure is not an option for me.
So you don't have to be sorry
and I don't need your charity.
Y'all just don't know my fight,
my pain, my sleepless nights, my testimony.
To tell the truth, I always had a little doubt.
Isn't that natural
I just never let it come out my mouth.
Everyday I'm reminded of the thing that left me behind
With plenty of time to myself
for the devil to corrupt my mind
And make me think I'm not good enough anyway.
and resent the people who have stood by me everyday.

Damn them all for not taking me along
For leaving me here with my frustration alone.

Remains To Be Seen

If you are just a little more patient and only believe in me
You would reap everything that remains to be seen.
Our little patch of love has sprouted past containment.
Being a control freak, I sabotaged us from the start.
Postponing the time for losing control of my heart.
Which can't be protected when it's in your hands
But, I can put up a hell of a fight, and that's what we have.
Uncertainty has me taking pieces of me back
It may not be right but it's what has happened,
those are the facts.
The truth, unlike what I told you.
And If I had to do it all over again,
I would have listened to you more and told you everything
from the beginning.
Couldn't see you wanted the best for me because I was
blinded by my own desires.
Even though I should, I'm still scared to let the old me retire.
But not too proud to tell you I'm sorry and mean it.
The tunnel is dark but the light is there,
it just remains to be seen.

You Saved Me

If it weren't for you, I don't know where I would be
Probably a mental institution, maybe six feet deep.
You saved me from allowing
that relationship to take over my life,
And from ignoring the signs
and making that woman my wife.
You saved me from getting drunk as a skunk
and not remembering the whole night
And from waking up early in the morning
and getting high as a kite.
You kept me from gossiping about people I don't even know.
I keep my opinions to myself. If it's not nice, I let it go.
You kept me from internalizing the opinions of others.
You saved me from being jealous of my sisters and brothers.
You took most of the crazy thoughts out of my head
Now I don't have to take all my opposite sex friends to bed.
You saved me from thinking
I got the rest of my life to get myself together,
And from always pointing the finger and blaming others for
things I brought on myself.
You saved me from riding under that 18 wheeler
when I fell asleep driving.
You saved me from getting robbed at the ATM that night.
You saved me from selfishness
and taught me to take others into consideration.
You taught me how to love, to be kind, gentle and patient.
You kept me from getting pregnant
and putting my dreams on hold.
When I left my keys in the car, you kept it from being stolen.
You kept me from going postal and going to jail.
You saved me from myself, you saved me from hell.
You saved my marriage, my children,
my reputation and my name.
You saved me from hatred, ridicule, and shame.
Even though I may not say thank You
and sometimes take You for granted,

I'll never forget when I was chopping up those vegetables and You kept me from cutting off my hand.

Pass the Test

If what doesn't kill me makes me stronger,
I'ma win the strongest man competition when this is over.
I'm exercising my brain with exponents,
square roots, and fractions.
Struggling to remember
formulas, equations, and chemical reactions.
It seemed like the test got harder
when they changed it to the computer format.
This is my fourth time taking it, don't I get credit for that.
At first when I should have been at the school studying,
I went home,
And instead of reading I was on the phone,
But in the last few weeks I practically bought stock in Starbucks,
Studied standing up and kept putting water on my face.
And around 1:37 a.m. I usually fall asleep
between the turn of every page.
Lord help me remember this information
and be able to apply the concepts.
Allow me to be focused on the day of the test.
This test isn't open book and we can't work in groups
They're watching us like hawks, they got us separated in booths.
You already promised me you wouldn't let me flunk
But after the last practice exam,
like a cotton shirt in the dryer, my confidence shrunk.
People keep saying, "You'll be alright, you'll pass the test?"
So will you at least allow me to stop doubting myself?
Lord, please help me remember this information and be able to
apply the concepts.
Allow me to be focused on the day of the test.
So even if my preparation wasn't the best
Or I happen to show up late to take the test;
Can you do what you've always done in the past?
I don't have to make an "A", just let me pass!

I'm Here Now

I barely have time to cook,
Lord knows I don't have time to play
And only a few hours of sleep separates the days.
But that's Ok because I beat the odds.
In college about to be a doctor,
the descendent of a slave and illiterate forefathers.
Who cares if I took the MCAT five times
and I'm thirty-eight
And the school lost all my paper work the second day?
All the time it took and the things I did to get here don't matter now.
He allowed me to make it, so I can't let Him down.
And even though I owe the school
more money than I've ever had
Until they drag me out, I'm coming to class
In scrubs on days I didn't even see the gross lab
Basking in my glory, smelling like formaldehyde.
Closer now than ever to the thing I've prayed for and waited on
for so long.
Wait until I tell the people at home.
They've been asking me about chronic symptoms and strange pains
since I was in undergrad.
I'd unintentionally kill a patient right now.
I'm not a doctor yet.
All I have to do now is get my in-class sleeping pose down
So it won't be so obvious when the professor is looking in my face
and
my head is bobbing around because I'm dozing off.
Is this what I signed up for?
trying to keep from drowning
In this pool of information, about the neck, hand and the facial layers
around it.
I'm here and I know that doesn't mean I've "arrived"
My tablet and clicker may not make it but, I will survive.
So for every one who didn't want to see me at my best
I'm here right now, I'm not there yet.

Weed State of Mind

"You did what? You said you wouldn't."
I know, I'm sorry, and it's not like I couldn't.
I feel retarded for saying what I'm so used to doing.
I've been smoking for 10 years and stopping for two,
It just hasn't come to fruition.

"What the hell does that mean?"
It means I like smoking weed
and never really wanted to stop.
I know it's bad for me but that's not what I was taught.
I can't fathom how many of my family members who smoke
I can count on two fingers the ones who don't.

"You will constantly be around weed."
Not really.
To think it can't be controlled is silly.
I understand it's something which you don't want to deal.
You won't have to deal with it. Please believe me, for real.
After going against my word,
I feel like there is nothing I can say.
I'm really surprised you're still here
after all the things you've said.

"I don't trust you
I have to question everything that you say"
Don't get me wrong, I'm glad you want what's best for me
and you've been patient
But if you feel like that,
you might as well hit the road today.
Without trust we don't have anything
and I can't imagine you would stay.
I hope you don't really feel that way.
And you see the good in me far outweighs the bad.
I would do anything for you, you can't force change.
Where do we go from here?
Can the trust be regained?

It will not take a long time.
To see my weed state of mind.

The Look in Your Eyes

The look in your eyes says it all.
I know that language well and quite frankly, I'm appalled
That you would undress me with a glance.
Hypnotize me with a smile and put me in a trance.
If you keep on looking at me the way you do
Others will begin to think that you want me too.
I know things can be misperceived
But in your eyes I see love for me.

Mama

Your love can't be matched even if it had a twin
A dictionary couldn't define our friendship
How do you tolerate me after all the nonsense?
I didn't deliberately disobey you,
Just trying to find my way.
And I love my sister even though
I fought with her every day.
You didn't have to whip me like you did.
The talks and looks you gave beat me down enough.
Because of you, I know what chivalry is
And just because I'm a man
doesn't mean to always act tough.
You showed me that "life ain't been no crystal stair"
And when it doesn't go like we plan
to smile and be glad that we're here.
I've never seen a person be so content with so little.
I know it ate you up inside, but you didn't let us know it.
God was using those situations to position us for something
greater.
I love you mama, I can't count the ways
You would beg, borrow, and steal
to fund my college education.
You made sure I knew how special I am
and to not spread myself too thin
You told me to use a condom
even when women told me they were on the pill.
You told me to stop smoking weed
but would hug me when I came home high.
You told me to be honest to women
because some of them are crazy and will hurt you
In the blink of an eye.
You told me you were proud of me
when I wasn't proud of myself.
You told me patience is a virtue
and cherish family until death.
With so many years under our belts,

it should be easy to express my emotions
But when I think of how wonderful you are,
I get choked up.

What Would You Do?

I would tell you I love you
But I'm not.
I would say it's too soon
But love doesn't go by a clock.
I would tell you I'm scared
But that wouldn't be me.
I would say there is no uncertainty
But I'd be lying.
I would say I could live without you
But inside I'd be dying.
What would you do if I told you?

Meet Me in My Dreams

Never in my dreams and not even in a million years
Did I imagine such a beautiful brown Queen.
It's like déjà vu every day.
This can't be real.
They don't write about love like this in songs or movie reels.
Don't be a mirage when I get close enough to hold you.
Don't disappear before I love you and remind you of all the
times I told you.
Instead, meet me in my dreams.
That way every night we can be together.
Meet me in my dreams, so we can dance barefoot on clouds as
soft as feathers.
Never wake me from our dream, I want to sleep forever.
Meet me in my dreams.

Fear

Can you imagine what it feels like to have your love?
Like warm wind beneath the wings of a dove.
Like a cool breeze after getting out of the tub.
I get chills.
That's only the beginning.
I can't imagine what it feels like to not see your smile.
Maybe like walking barefoot on glass for miles.
Torture.
When I see your teeth pierce your lips it's all solved.
Scariness disappears and uncertainty dissolved.
But only until the accuser appears and picks at scars
Of a wounded soldier trapped behind bars.
With the fear of being played
From what I used to do right in your face.

God Is

My rock, my love, the Prince of Peace
My soul, my heart, my unborn niece
My joy, my pain, my happiness and contentment
My provider, my nourishment and money for rent
My Savior, my Lord, my light
My tears of joy and the ones I try to fight
Wonderful counselor, my strength, my guide
My accountant, my manager, my head and by my side
The purpose of my life and my death
My Shepherd, The King, my help
My physician, my voice, my health
My next move and my every step
My mom, my dad, my sister, my brother
My home, my covering
My heat, my cold, my right and my left
My check before bills and whatever is left
God is my everything.

A Tiger Wearing One Sock

Constant thoughts of you clog my brain every season.
When you're not by my side, I can still see you cheesing.
If you add up all the fun we've had
and all the words I've spoken
You'd see our love is extra full, it's bloated.
Overflowing like a tub filled with red Kool-Aid
Running like a doe from the end of her days.
Reaching you no matter where you're staying
Without constraints because it can't be tamed.
Without a label to put it in a box
Running wild like a tiger wearing one sock,
Unexplainable.

Without Reservation, Doubt, or Fear

I have loved you forever in one lifetime.
If I don't live another second, I'll be satisfied.
Knowing only a remnant of love.
I would never underestimate you or take you for granted.
And never forsake the seeds of intimacy that we've planted.
Don't be afraid of uncertainty, It's what makes life fun.
Fear and doubt are likely companions.
It seems like days are nights and nights are days,
Timelessness, lost in your eyes when I look in your face.
Brown skin, the color of cinnamon
A delicacy like no other
Two days and three nights is almost not enough
To know Love.
Though it tarry, wait for it to appear.
Without reservation, doubt, or fear
All unlikely emotions for something I hold so dear.
We missed the narrow gate and forced our own path
Landing right outside the promised land
With no account of what brought us here.
Without reservation, doubt, or fear.

Redefine Love and Laugh All Night

The Lord created the world in six days
And used specific words to describe our devotion,
like true and amazing.
He's not done building it up
And we haven't seen a fraction of His glory
I pray I'm reincarnated as our love story.
Grace me with your presence by my side
As we enjoy the ride of our lives.
Let's redefine love and laugh all night.
Play scrabble till we fall asleep
and dance when no one is in sight
Hold my hand and display our love for the world to see
In Tennessee, on a trolley in Paris,
or tropical jungles in Belize.
Relieved to have a compliment to me
We matched, your random ridiculousness is my blessing.
So on this day of the ride of our lives
Let's redefine love and laugh all night.
Evade the frost of disappointment in my arms.
As we're held by the Lord and kept from harm.
May He bless our adoration and set it apart
May we only be separated when there are no beats left in
either one of our hearts.
May our affection advance from the first day we walk on rice.
Let's redefine love and laugh all night.

On the Edge

Is it really possible to love like this?
Maybe I just don't know what love is.
I told God when He sent me you,
I'd pledge to worship the ground you walk on
and when you're tired to massage your legs.
When we're laughing it up and especially when I'm trying to
pull you back from the edge.
Even when we both put on weight
and long after the roses I buy you are dead.
I'll laugh when I think about the time I rented a sports car
to speed off the ledge
To end up in the abyss of resentment,
where our relationship lay lifeless, dead.
When I didn't know if I wanted to be around you
for the next thirty minutes
Never mind being around long enough to have kids.
And It was nothing you did and certainly nothing you said
But suddenly I found myself stepping back from the edge.

You Never Told Me

I know what Love is!
No thanks to you.
I'm not saying you don't love me,
You just don't know what to do.
When an ounce of love does come from you
I can't help but remember the daily beating and the bruises.
Is it the guilt that got you being so nice;
Or do you want to get close enough to my back with a knife?
Was I everything you ever dreamed of being,
Or were you trying to steal my joy from me?
After all these years I finally see,
You were jealous of the relationship between me and my
daddy.
The Lord only knows if any of the past matters.
You're my mother until the fat lady sings and the last
Champaign glass gets shattered.
How our relationship unfolds, we're all going to see.
I guess what I'm trying to say is…
I love you.
Even though I'm your daughter and you never told me.

The Ship

All aboard!
The first thing smoking.
You don't have to pay,
You don't even need tokens.
But in order to ride, you have to be all the way on.
It's a one-way trip, lets embark and take off.
Check your baggage by checking yourself.
I wouldn't be going if I didn't think we could
make it together.
Our friendship means a lot because I don't have that many
And I have trust issues, know that from the beginning.
It doesn't matter if the water gets choppy
and we get hurricane warnings
Or we lose communication with the people guiding us home.
Water could fill the keel, the entire hull and we could capsize
We could go down like the Titanic,
we know we're about to die.
But I'm not going anywhere; I'm going down with the ship.
Is our relationship strong enough or would you jump?
We can take turns at the helm,
I don't have to be captain.

Broke Ambition

She didn't see any determination in his eyes
Defeat swallowed her simple man
Trying hard never moved so slow
Nothing he did in this life is worth it.
One time he stole a guitar and let it sit in the corner
Then took up surfing and alligator trapping
At one time he wanted to be an astronaut
But spent all the money he saved for space camp.
Aggravation stains his wrinkle-filled forehead.
Nothing seems to work.
He feels so low.
Blind ambition broke him.

Can't Nobody/Wouldn't If They Could

Can't nobody do me like you.
Doubt they would if they could
Take time to get to know the real me and
Patiently explain until things are understood.
It was official when,
My pockets were empty and couldn't call on my "friends".
You gave me everything
And didn't tell me I'm just like the other ones.
I cheated on you, cussed you out, and acted a fool.
You took me back with no problem.
Who else would do me like you?
Never made me feel bad about who I am;
Just held me tight, rubbed my back
Wiped my tears and asked
For nothing in return.
After you showed me the way and told me how to go.
I embraced immaturity and nurtured lack
Then prayed for you to show up.
The frustration never left a mark on your face.
Even though jealousy has always been
one of your strong traits,
Can't nobody do me like you.
Nope.
Wouldn't if they could
Play silly board games, laugh til they love me and
Patiently explain until things are understood.

Comfort Zone

Couldn't see until it was almost too late
Told myself I was staying for the kids
But was really digging myself an early grave
Staying in my comfort zone because I was afraid
Of the unknown.
You halfway know the devil you got,
Have no clue about the one you're going to get
Does that mean remain here in this nonsense
In a comfort zone that's not so comfortable
Can't count the number of names I've been called
The embarrassing comments, the dreams I stalled
And even though I have to walk with my head down
To feel no shame
I stay.
Tired of playing the dating game so
I remain
Here defeated.
How can something so bad, hurt so good?
One kiss from her soft, full lips, and I forget my name.
I don't need a name in the intimate places she takes me.
Call me Kunta and cut my foot off if I try to leave.
Call me her love slave
Because of the gentleness she sometimes displays.
It's a shame because sex only lasts for so long
And I'm back in our comfort zone.
Fooling myself into staying
Afraid of the unknown, afraid of
Being
Alone
Digging myself an early grave
Staying in my comfort zone.

For So Long

Anxiously waiting on you to show up
Where have you been all my life?
After delusion and dehydration, I find my oasis.
Don't dry up before this memory can forever be retained.
And I can live hereafter in your veins.
When you came so abruptly
My wall was still up
Still scared to feel.
Now's the chance to see what real love is
With no limitations and no fear.
I'll protect you from the evil in the world that is
For as long as the time we have here.
I've been waiting too long to neglect my duty
and make careless mistakes
My love won't be that unpredictable.
It will be shown with no hesitation
For so long.

God's Response (Answer to Why Me)

Do you believe I won't forsake nor leave you?
I'm incapable of lying. Know the truth.
Proud of you since before coming into existence.
I made you just like Me.
You have the power to heal yourself, break strongholds and be free.
Love others like yourself and let Me handle the rest.
It pleases Me to give you the world,
just be cool and pass a few tests.
No weapon, trial, or person formed against you shall prosper, only fail.
And no height, depth, or creature can separate us,
not even the devil in hell.
I take care of you even when you don't do what I say
But a long life, full of peace I give to those who obey.
All my ways are loving and faithful,
I care to know the number of hairs on your head and face
So I give you joy, patience, kindness, and peace.
Well done faithful servant, in whom I am well pleased.

How Did We Get Here?

How did trivial things grow high, long, wide and in between
Have you crying and me being mean?
Was my punishment meant for the men in your past?
Is being me good enough to be in your class?
My background might be shaky, but its mine.
Too much baggage is slowing down this journey of ours.
You never trusted me enough to commit.
Probably because of how things were in the beginning.
Walking out on you every chance I got,
Avoiding every conversation that involved me changing.
How did we get to this place,
Me being mean and that look on your face?
We talked about it last night, you want to talk about it again
Our time is short and my patience is thin.
We both know but have different views of what love is.
That's how this mole hill turned into a mountain
And made you reverse 10 steps
Every time you did, I took back a part of myself
That's how we got to this place.
You charged me up saying
"Go on leave, you want to do it anyway."
If you wanted me to stay, why would you push me away?
To control the situation, I became extra tough.
Instead of protecting you and building you up
When you finally "came around," in my mind, it was too late.
That's how we got to this place.

If They Only Knew

All over the place is he and she.
Not knowing what is and not believing what's seen.
Here and now is where they are to be
Instead of watching stagnant emotions
grow bacteria and form disease.
Asked not what to do or say
And can't be asked not to feel some kind of way.
If they only knew what was in store
Would they hit the road or walk through the open door.
Patience is nurtured like an only beloved son.
He's over himself and tired of "having fun."
Given freely is the time they need
Here for her is he, if she waits to see.
Never angrily walking out another door
Nor applying pressure to know what's in store.
If they only knew.
His left hand is telling him to talk to her
On the other, it says she can't handle the truth.
Words are picked like good from rotten fruit
Telling half the story is
Not telling the truth
If they only knew.

What If/ I Wish

What if there was no such thing as free will?
It was just called destruction.
I wish God didn't let us do whatever we wanted.
I wish it was easier for me to live righteous.
What if the devil never noticed me,
Would I be less able to fight mess?
I wish I would have listened to all the things my momma
told me.
What if I didn't need affirmation or a woman to hold me?
What if I could take back all the bad things I've uttered?
Would you listen or think about all the times I was harsh;
Be defensive and regurgitate a few choice curse words?
What if we had more time, more patience, and more real
friends?
What if people weren't so easily entertained?
I'm not sure if I wish there were more hours in every day.
What if my people didn't think being stylish meant dressing
like a pimp?
What if the fire that burned within me was extinguished,
And I swam like a rock, and flew like a penguin?
What if all my wishes came true?
I wish I would know what to do.

Let's Do It

Let's do it like it's going out of style
On the 1,080th hour of the year
Let's do it like Houdini, with magic, then disappear.
Let's do it like the bees and the birds.
Let's do it like some computer hacking nerds.
Let's do it like I'm just coming back from war.
Like you're happier to see me now than you were before.
Like when I didn't know what to do, so I pulled your hair
And wanted to be where you were so I raced you there.
This Valentine's day, I've been counting down the seconds
Until you run into my arms and kiss me before catching
your
breath.
Let's do it like kids do, without fear.
Let's enjoy the time we have here.

Miss You Already

Ok, one more time.
When are you leaving and coming back?
How long the time is without my love.
Every second ushers the moment until you hurry back
Which never comes fast enough.
Before you get on the plane and it takes off,
Before the wings get up in the air and steady,
Before you buy your flight reading material,
I miss you already.
Before you get settled in your hotel,
Before finding out how many missed calls you have
I've been having conversations with you in my head
Before you even left
Because I miss you already.
Before you get on the plane and it takes off
Before the wings get steady
Before you open your flight-reading material
I miss you already.

New Beginning

It's not the end, just a new beginning
Besides wrong, who knows what we would have been.
Letting two minutes of pleasure ruin everything
Instead of focusing on our dreams
Thoughts of you won't leave my mind
Your witty comments, long feet, and thick thighs
Your tattoo, belly ring, sweet smell and intense eyes.
Why are we not doing this one more time?
God has a plan for you, a super-sized surprise
As long as you're concerned about what's done in His eyes
It's not the end, just a new beginning
Who knows what is, but has not been.

Sweet Thang

Sounding like candy and tasting like roses,
It seems insane but it's not.
Confused by your spiciness and sweet soul,
If that means having schizophrenic senses,
that's what I got.
Playing crazy if it means having my boo,
Voices keep screaming, "Hold on to that girl."
Create a kingdom with her in the center.
Give it all up so everything can be gained,
Just so I can call you my sweet thang.

The Most Beautifulest!

You are the most beautifulest thing that has ever been seen
By me or anybody else.
Not to mention how much you compliment me
And that's not the only thing that attracts me to yourself.
Ever catch me staring when you're around?
The focus is not just on your butt.
I'm admiring and thinking of ways to keep you around
And...I'm looking at...other stuff.
Like the dark black hair that outlines your gorgeous face
All your features right where they're supposed to be.
When you need a perm, that hair at the top
stays in one place.
You could be bald and still be astonishing.
Like when spring brings green leaves to trees
Or when rose pedals lean over, offering raindrops a seat
Like a traditional ceremonial dance to bring peace
The most beautifulest thing that has ever been seen.
Perfectly proportioned,
Never seen anything like it
Nothing in the world made, bought, or sold can deny it.
No thing is comparable in right.
Because you are easily the most beautifulest thing that has
ever been seen
By me or anybody else.

Wonderful

When did being smart, kind, generous and fun become not enough?

Once God made you absolutely stunning and a whole lot of other stuff

Never have I ever seen a woman so divine

Defined, desirable, and one of a kind.

Ever wonder what happened to the mold used to make you? He broke it!

Right after forming the most magnificent creature alive,

Faithfully fulfilling my destiny by making you mine.

Uncanny how someone so wonderful would end up with simple me,

Loving you from now until infinity!

The Truth

I might be a new creature but my old self stays on the scene.
Death comes with caring more about what people think
than what God sees in me.
As I reluctantly travel down a road
far from where I aim to be,
I run with my eyes closed
trying to resist the devil, hoping he will flee.
If God hadn't saved me from myself,
I would have been dead.
The truth is, I brushed my shoulders off
and acted like I saved me, instead.
My pride got in the way after medical school.
I straddled that line between being brutally honest and being
an inconsiderate fool
Until I found out only a remnant of us might be saved,
though we outnumber the sand by the sea.
The truth is,
Miracles aren't enough for some of us to believe.
The fake is flamboyant, in your face, and on every corner.
The truth is hidden in between the lines
collecting dust in a corner.
I may have missed out on a lot of blessings
Too stubborn to change.
If I get what I'm supposed to have,
did I really miss out on anything?
My hand has already been dealt,
He's just watching to see how I play it.
I just hope my sins aren't enough to keep me outside the
gates.

Excerpt from Lamont's Novel

We finally made it to Pantherburn, Mississippi. It was eight and a half square miles of sticks and leaves, about two hours northwest of Jackson. The whole town probably never had more than 200 people in it at one time. That meant if you peed on the side of a building, they would be talking about it in Sunday school. Everybody knew everybody, which wasn't a good thing all the time.

My grandfather, known as "Jack the Bear" to everyone else, left my grandmother and moved to the Delta after he got her pregnant for the twelfth time. He probably had kids in every town in the Delta. His death was kind of a surprise because he was very active on the farm and was healthier at seventy-six than people half his age. The word was the doctors gave him a heart attack. They messed his medicine up. Trying to get information out of the Pantherburn family was harder than Japanese arithmetic. Somebody knew something, but they weren't telling. Nobody talked about malpractice, but everybody talked about insurance money. The average annual income in Pantherburn was about $12,000. The policy couldn't have been more than $300.

We pulled up to The Bear's street a little after twelve p.m. People were parked everywhere. The H2 limo couldn't make it down the narrow street. That meant a nice dusty walk to the yellow wood siding house Bear used to live in. Most of the front yard was dirt, hardly any grass. There was a hibernating garden in the backyard ready to come to life after the spring rain.

"Vera, we don't need no mess out of you. We don't want to hear nothing about how dad ain't never been no good and especially nothing about getting some insurance money. If he didn't give you anything when he was alive, he sure isn't giving you anything now." That was my father, Kendall Trevin Robinson Sr. He tried to keep the peace. He tried.

"I bet you don't," Aunt Vera slurred right before sucking the last corner out of her pint sized bottle of Hennessy.

"Madear, you gone be alright in the limo for a minute or you want to come in?" I kind of shouted because she could barely hear. Madear grabbed my arm with her fragile, shaking hands.

She smiled and winked her right eye as she whispered "Bring me a beer."

It took me twenty-two years to realize my great grandmother had blue eyes. It sounds funny, but for twenty-two years I never noticed. I was so busy living my life, running the streets, and being off at school, that I never really took the opportunity to sit down, look into her face and pay attention. Massa must have been doing something wrong. She was the only dark skinned black person I knew with blue eyes. She probably told somebody else to get her one too. That might have been her secret to living so long.

We got out of the limo and we walked up to the screen door with no screen.

"I hope they got some food in there," huffed Aunt Sharon.

"You always hungry," said Vera.

"And you always drunk," Sharon retaliated.

Ruth's house was packed from wall to wall. There was standing room only on the worn-down maroon carpet. The house was smaller on the inside than it looked from the outside. I'm sure it brought Vera comfort to know her father didn't give his other kids more than he gave her.

Most of the people were talking about Bear and the good old days. Everybody who wasn't talking was eating. I thought people were supposed to eat after the funeral. We walked toward Ruth. She had her feet halfway propped up in the dark green recliner Bear used to sit in. She was halfway listening to people tell her how sorry they were for her loss.

Ruth was a slim dark skinned woman with a round face and short hair. She had on a fuchsia suit. It was almost red. She didn't look like she was grieving to me. She had her fingers buried in some greens and cornbread. She stopped sucking her fingers and chewing long enough to situate the food in her mouth and say "Y'all made it huh?"

"I came especially to give you a piece of my-"

My father yanked Vera's arm in mid sentence and almost pulled her down to the floor. Her balance was already off.

Ruth stopped eating, sat her flimsy paper plate on the end table and stood up.

"Everybody, everybody, let's go." Ruth made the announcement after ignoring Vera. The people in the house didn't respond fast enough for Ruth so she stuck two fingers in her mouth and whistled like she was trying to call a dog up the street. Most of the conversations came to a hault.

"I'm ready," she practically whispered.

It was one thing to be ghetto. It was another to be country. It was unfortunate to be both. As everyone filed out of the house, I went toward the refrigerator. There were empty pots, pans, and other dishes all over the kitchen which was smaller than the closet in Angela's guestroom. I opened the fridge and saw three Milwaukee's Best right on the top shelf. Madear's favorite. Every beer was her favorite. I grabbed one and put it inside my suit jacket pocket. Ruth watched me close the refrigerator door. I wondered if she saw me put the beer in my pocket. I wasn't stealing, I didn't think. I walked out of the house behind everybody else.

It had begun to drizzle and small raindrops were accumulating on my glasses. My father was standing next to the chauffer under an umbrella watching me walk up.

"I hope you weren't getting food." He told me.

"That's how she got your Granddaddy, put something in his food."

My dad was one of the few people I knew who believed in voodoo. He actually believed someone could put something in your food to make you fall in love with them or make you lose your mind. Sometimes losing your mind and falling in love where one in the same.

The church where the funeral was held was deeper in the country. Ebenezer Holiness Missionary Baptist Church was at the end of a rocky, dirt road that had patches of grass between the tire tracks. The patches of grass on the road to the church let you know that road was the one less traveled. There was no grass anywhere around a crack house.

"Enter through the narrow gate. For wide is the gate and broad is the road that leads to destruction, and many enter through it. But small is the gate and narrow the road that leads to life, and few find it." Matthew 7:13-14

Most of the people parked on the wet grass or along the road that led to the church. That made the narrow road even narrower. The cold wind frosted noses and ears as we formed the procession to follow the casket into the church. The gray and black ominous clouds released raindrops that got bigger by the second. Flashes of lightening illuminated the sky in the distance followed by loud bursts of thunder that sounded too close for comfort.

Every expense was spared on this funeral and it was easy to tell from the beginning. The hearse wasn't even a hearse. It was an El Camino with a homemade wooden camper covering the back. There was no family car for the immediate family to ride in. Only three people came from the funeral home to conduct the funeral and one of them had on a baby blue Zoot Suit. The jacket dropped down to his knees, which may not have been so ridiculous if he was pimping at the club. He was supposed to have on black to work at a funeral. It was 2010, not 1940. The funeral home immediately put the pall-bearers to wok getting them to help put Bear's casket onto the wheeled casket stand. Jack the Bear was about 6'2" and almost 300 lbs. That's how he got his name.

We began to slowly march into the church. People were already crying. I didn't want people to cry for me at my funeral. You don't cry for somebody who's in paradise. It was always hard to tell if people were crying because they were hurt or because of their own selfishness; because they felt bad about the unresolved issue between them and the person or they didn't have their hang out buddy anymore.

When they got to the front of the church with the casket, they tried to turn it around to put it in position for viewing. As they tried to make the turn, a wheel came loose or something wasn't set up right because the casket stand folded up like a lawn chair and the casket almost hit the ground.

You should have seen them struggling to keep the top closed and the casket up. People gasped as others ran over to help stabilize the coffin. I knew right then, I should have taken my camera out.

I didn't know anything about an insurance policy, but I did know Bear used to keep a pocket full of hundred dollar bills. He may have pinched the money out so no one would know how much he had, but it seemed like all he had to pinch out was hundred dollar bills. The bad thing about it was they could have thrown him in a hole under that raggedy garden at his house and saved the paper for the obituary. It wouldn't have made too much of a difference. He was dead and I didn't know who he was when he was alive. He wasn't the type of grandfather who came around to give you candy and tell you stories. It usually didn't matter if the stories were the truth or not. He didn't drop off a few dollars and tell you not to spend it all in one place. Whatever else grandfathers did, he didn't do it.

We finally got seated. The small church got full quick. People were up against the wall shaking off umbrellas and sneezing. There were adults and babies crying. The Bear had sown so many wild oats, I wouldn't have been surprised if I was related to everybody there.

The people who drove from Jackson took up almost two pews. My uncles and aunts hardly ever went to see Bear when he was alive and found stuff to do when he did come to Jackson to visit them. Some of the youngest of his children didn't know him that well because he didn't stick around long after they were born and didn't start visiting until the last few years of his life. Why do people wait until the end of life to make amends?

How do you accept a man as a father who has never been there for you? He may as well be some random man on the street. The preacher was a dark man with big prominent features, especially his nose and teeth. He moved slowly, but not from fatigue. It was cool, calm and collected. When he got to the podium, he was quiet for a minute as he overlooked the congregation.

The preacher started. "Let us pray. Dear Heavenly, and gracious Father. We are gathered here today in a celebration of Brother Jack's home going. You say in Your word that we should rejoice at death and weep at birth. Father God we ask that you be with the family in this time of their searching for answers. Let them know that Brother Jack is without hurt and pain, Lord, away from the evil and corruption of this world. Let me be used as a vessel to bring forth your word and let anything that is said glorify your name. In your darling son

Jesus name we pray. Amen." He went on to say "Now we will have a selection by the Ebenezer Holiness Church choir."

The choir began its rendition of Amazing Grace. It didn't matter who sang that song or how they sang it, it usually brought tears to my eyes. I couldn't help but think about how blessed I was. I sang along. "How sweet the sound, that saved a wretch like me. I once was lost, but now am found, was blind but now I see." Then they started singing a lesser known verse.

"Through many dangers toil and snares I have already come. T'was grace that brought me safe thus far and grace will lead me home."

Everywhere I went, I observed people whether I was at church or in line at AutoZone. You would be amazed at what you saw if you paid attention. Most people couldn't hide being happy, upset, excited, or the look of smelling something funky. Watching adults could be redundant, children were enlightening. I wasn't looking for anything in particular. People just fascinated me. Just by looking at a person, you could never tell what they were thinking, why they thought it or what they had been through. If you listened, they told you everything you wanted to know and half the stuff you didn't want to know. Sometimes you just had to use your decoder.

There was a little girl sitting in front of me who had to be the youngest person with a jheri curl ever. There should have been an age limit on Jheri Curls. There were a couple of noticeably gay choir members singing their hearts out. They needed Jesus like all the other sinners in church. Lord knows I had done enough wrong in my life to go to hell a couple times. "For all have sinned and fall short of the glory of God." Romans 3:23

"Now we will hear briefly from anyone who wants to say a few words about Brother Jack," the preacher said.

There was a brown skinned man standing at the front of the church, probably a deacon. He was bald in the top of his head and had a jheri curl on the sides. Apparently he was in denial about his baldness because he had strands of his curl pulled across the top to try to cover his bald spot. It wasn't working.

The man stood up and said "Nothing we say right now will help or hurt brother Jack the Bear."

Ruth was on the front row clipping her nails, digging in her purse and doing everything else but mourning.

"I loveded brother Bear," the deacon went on to say. "And I believe he loveded me. There was nothing he wouldn't do for me or anybody else if they askeded him. I knowed him pretty good after he moved to the Delta and there was times when he was the onliest one I could count on. He was a good man."

"We at the wrong funeral. I know he not talking about the Bear?" uncle Duck said from the row behind me. The deacon may have been telling the truth. It's possible that Jack the Bear had turned over a new leaf or camouflaged the old one.

Then the only person we didn't want to speak stood up. Vera gathered herself and began.

"My momma-"

"Would you like to come to the front?" the preacher asked.

Vera got her balance before screaming, "That's alright. I might not make it. My momma, Jack's first wife, had 12 kids by this dead man. It was a lot of us. We had it bad. Mama had to clean houses and do whatever she had to do to take care of all of us. We had to sleep on top of each other almost four and five to a bed but she made sure we ate even if it wasn't nothing but wish meat sandwiches. Y'all know what wish meat is? It's bread, you wish you had some meat. One day she finally broke down and decided to ask the Bear for some help. She took Big K with her down to the Delta. I don't know why she took him, he was the baddest and he was always crying, but that don't matter. 'The kids are hungry Jack.' she told him. 'Tell them to put their fingers in their mouths.' Bear replied with Big K standing right there. Big K will tell you."

They called my dad Big K and called me Lil K or Tre when they felt like it. My father didn't say a word but he and several of his brothers and sisters nodded their heads. Vera went on. "Momma talked him into selling us a goat. For whatever reason, he couldn't give us a goat out of the ones he owned. When Mama brought that raggedy goat out the trunk, you should have seen the look on our faces. I had seen several goats before but not like that one. That goat had a limp like a pimp and had patches of hair missing like it had been fighting other Billy goats. We didn't see our daddy that much and that's what I remember."

I heard that story several times from different family members before I actually met my grandfather. It was his legacy. I don't think they ever forgave him for that. Everybody else who talked at the funeral "loveded" brother Bear, let them tell it. I guess the funeral wasn't a good time to dig up an old grave or say 'He oweded me five dollars or ten ears of corn' or something like that. I heard the mispronunciation of so many words it was frightening. Some people thought southerners were slow and stupid because we talked a little slow or used words we made up. The truth was a lot of us were uneducated. Some because we had to start working early to provide for our families and others because the education offered to poor black people could barely be considered basic. Mississippi had one of the lowest rankings associated with Education. It wasn't by chance, it was intentional. Almost ninety years ago, if a nigger did try to learn to read, he got hung or beat half to death. Blacks were never expected to be educated so the resources used to educate us were inferior to say the least.

Right before it was time to view the body, Ruth's oldest daughter Janice stood up in front of Ruth and started fanning her. That must have been Ruth's cue because a few seconds later Janice was picking Ruth up from the floor. They walked out the church without viewing the body and without saying a word. They didn't make it to the burial site.

My grandfather was a brown skinned man with short salt and pepper hair on the sides, mostly salt. He was bald in the top and his skin looked a little pale. They did a good job on him, it looked like he was smiling in his sleep. I never thought I looked like my father until I realized how much my father looked like my grandfather. My father's facial expression didn't change from the time we got there until the time we left, not even when Aunt Vera cleared her throat every time people said good things about the Bear. Nothing we said could help or hurt Jack the Bear. He was gone to the "upper room."

200 Months of Rain

Spoken Words by Lamont

Lamont

TrueVinePublishing.org